Linda Hammant
32 Rochester Avenue
Rochester

THE BASSET HOUND

JOAN WELLS-MEACHAM

Illustrations by Ishbel Macdonald

John Bartholomew & Son Limited
Edinburgh

First published in Great Britain 1980 by
JOHN BARTHOLOMEW & SON LIMITED
12 Duncan Street, Edinburgh EH9 1TA

© John Bartholomew & Son Limited 1980

All rights reserved. No part of this publication may be reproduced, stored in a retrieval system, or transmitted, in any form, or by any means, electronic, mechanical, photocopying, recording, or otherwise, without the prior permission of John Bartholomew & Son Limited.

ISBN 0 7028 8390 5

British Library Cataloguing in Publication Data

Wells-Meacham, Joan
   The basset hound. – (Bartholomew pet series).
   1. Basset-hounds
   I. Title
   636.7'53   SF429.B2

Printed in Great Britain by
John Bartholomew & Son Limited, Edinburgh

Contents

	Page
Breed History	7
The Breed Standard	14
Choosing a Puppy	23
Housing and Training	29
Exhibiting	37
Your Dog's Health	43
Breeding	49
The Hunting Basset	58
The Basset Hound in America	66
Index	76

Introduction

I have endeavoured to write this book with the novice owner in mind in an attempt to answer the sort of questions I have been asked on many occasions. I have therefore avoided, as far as possible, the use of technical terms and involvement in the scientific aspects of breeding and puppy-rearing. It will be readily apparent to readers that this book is not intended as a text-book for the established breeder.

I would like to acknowledge the help I have received from Mr Evan Roberts in the compilation of this book; also Mr Michael Dennis for his contribution to the chapter on hunting.

Head of the Basset Hound

One: Breed History

The precise origin of the Basset Hound is uncertain but French authorities of the sixteenth and seventeenth centuries agree on Artois and Flanders as the probable home of the breed. Its ancestors would appear to include the Talbot, Sleuth Hound and perhaps, most important, the St. Hubert Hound bred in the monastery of St. Hubert and contributed annually to the French royal kennels. The latter were apparently large hounds used for hunting the larger game such as wild boar, but in time, as smaller game began to attract the attention of the hunter, so smaller hounds were developed from which the modern Basset Hound probably stems.

The name Basset simply indicates that the hound is low to the ground and one of the third group of hounds recognised by French huntsmen – those between 10 and 15 inches at the shoulder. The modern French Basset exists in various forms, the main distinctions lying in the degree of crook in the forelegs and the nature of the coat.

Of the four varieties of Basset recognised in France, the most important from our point of view is the Basset Artesian Normand, as the first Bassets imported into this country in the nineteenth century were of this type. This variety was developed mainly by Le Comte Le Coulteaux de Canteleu and Monsieur Lane as the result of crossing the practically extinct Artesian strain with the more prolific Normand. These two strains differed mainly in the formation and hang of the leathers, the Artesian Basset's ears having a curled or corkscrew appearance as opposed to the flat hand of the Normand's. Le Coulteaux-bred hounds tended to be lighter in bone than the Lane type, the latter usually having a broader skull and bolder eye. As regards fronts the Lane type usually had a greater degree of crook.

The other smooth-coated variety is the Basset Bleu de Gascoigne which is larger than the Artesian Normand and is attractively marked with black patches on a blue mottled background.

The rough-coated varieties are the Basset Griffon Vendeen and the Basset Fouve de Bretagne, the latter usually being smaller and of a distinctive wheaten or fawn colour with patches on occasion.

In 1866 a brace of Bassets of the Artesian Normand variety was imported into England by Lord Galway. These hounds 'Basset' and 'Belle' were tricolours of the Canteleu type and when mated in 1867 produced a litter of five. Subsequently in 1872, Lord Galway was able to sell seven dogs to the Earl of Onslow, who augmented his pack by importing further Le Canteleu hounds until it numbered fourteen or fifteen couples.

In about 1882 he, in turn, sold his entire pack to Sir Everett Millais and Mr G R Krehl.

In the meantime, Sir Everett Millais had himself imported a Basset – 'Model' – in 1874 which he exhibited at Wolverhampton and London in 1875 winning on each occasion in variety classes. 'Model' was mated to one of the original Onslow hounds and most Bassets in England today are descended from these strains though further imports were made by Mr Krehl and Mr Clements. By 1880 the breed was fairly well established in England and in that year, breed classes were provided for the first time at Wolverhampton.

It will be seen, therefore, that the Basset in England today is descended mainly from the Artesian-Normand strain, more particularly the Le Canteleu type though some Lane elements

Basset Hound at rest

were very probably introduced in the later 1880s and it is still possible today to distinguish on occasion the distinctive characteristics of the two types mentioned above.

Turning to the Basset's uses, it will become apparent that this hound has not always been used in the same manner, there being a marked distinction between French and English methods.

Originally, in France, Bassets were used rather as working terriers are used today, going to ground after fox and badger. For this work the crooked forelegs were an advantage although limiting the hound's speed above ground.

Nowadays, however, the Basset is used mainly for driving game of all types and it is interesting to conjecture that this change may well have come about through some Bassets with straighter fronts being found to be better above ground than below without being actually fast enough to catch the game.

Today in France when they are used on a shoot, they work with the beaters driving the game towards the guns at a reasonable pace thus giving a reasonable chance for a kill. The guns are stationed at suitable points for the game to break cover being guided by the hounds as they work through the thickets. In connection with this it is appropriate to mention at this point that the Basset has perhaps the most musical voice of all hounds and it is a real joy to the hunting enthusiast to listen to this hound giving tongue.

Of course, the Basset's short legs make its acute scenting powers even more effective compared with the longer-legged scent hounds and it has even been suggested that the Basset's long ears brushing through the grass or vegetation bring up the scent, but this must remain a matter for speculation.

In the United States of America Bassets are widely used both for hunting the hare as in England and for driving game towards guns. In addition, they have also been used successfully rather as gundogs are used in England for trailing, flushing and retrieving birds such as pheasant.

It must be clear that some of the Basset's characteristics, particularly the crooked forelegs, can put the breed at a disadvantage in the hunting field compared with lighter, speedier hounds and this has led during the present century to something of a split between those who breed primarily for show and those whose main interest lies primarily in the hunting field. Many packs hunting with 'Bassets' today in fact make use of varying types involving out-crossing with other hound breeds to produce mainly longer and straighter legs, while still maintaining the beautiful voice of the Basset, the name 'English Basset' being used to describe these various types.

With the increasing popularity of the breed in the nineteenth century, there was an obvious need for an organisation to look after and further the interests of the breed and this led in 1884 to the formation of the Basset Hounds Club, the hunting interests being catered for by the Masters of Basset Hounds Association formed in 1911. The Club was disbanded due to lack of support in 1921 but re-formed in 1954, since when it has prospered, having now about five hundred members. In 1957 the Club widened its scope by forming a Working Branch to cater for members interested in hunting with the pure-bred Basset. The Masters of Basset Hounds Association, having also been disbanded, was re-formed in 1958.

The increasing popularity of the breed has been shown by the increase in registrations at the Kennel Club from thirteen in 1930 to a peak of over two thousand in 1967. At present about four hundred puppies are registered annually.

As registrations increased in number, classes for Bassets at Championship Shows were increasingly well-supported and perhaps the first notable post-war show landmark was when Mrs Jennifer Townson's Champion Rossingham Badger was Reserve Best in Show at Windsor in 1958. A grandson of this hound, namely, my own Champion Fredwell Varon Vandal

Tricolour Basset Hound

began his outstanding show career in 1960. During that year he won twenty-three Challenge Certificates all under different judges including foreign specialists and created a record for the breed. In referring to these hounds one should also record with gratitude the work of Miss M M Keevil who did so much to keep the breed going during the difficult war time and immediate post-war years and whose Grims Hounds are behind today's top winners. The Club Pack was formed with Miss Keevil's help and with the loan of her hounds.

Today, a typical Basset tends on the whole to be rather less heavily built than his forebears, to have lost some of the old Bloodhound head characteristics and to have a somewhat less accentuated crook. One feels, however, that feet have improved greatly, far fewer flat, splayed or hare-feet being evident now and that there is much more correlation between appearance and soundness. Most winning hounds today exhibit a balanced combination of sound front and hindquarters, deep body coupled with a true topline, good head qualities and an ability to move with drive and purpose.

Two: The Breed Standard

General characteristics
A short-legged hound of considerable substance, well-balanced and full of quality. Action is most important. A smooth, free action with forelegs reaching well forward and hind legs showing powerful thrust and the hound moving true both front and rear. Hocks and stifles must not be stiff in movement nor must any toes be dragged.

Head and Skull
Domed with some stop and the occipital bone prominent; of medium width at the brow and tapering slightly to the muzzle;

the general appearance of the foreface is lean but not snipy. The top of the muzzle nearly parallel with the line from the stop to the occiput and not much longer than the head from stop to occiput. There may be a moderate amount of wrinkle at the brows and beside the eyes and in any event the skin of the head should be so loose as to wrinkle noticeably when drawn forward or when the head is lowered. The flews of the upper lip overlap the lower substantially.

Nose
Entirely black, except in light-coloured hounds, when it may be brown or liver. Large with well-opened nostrils and may protrude a little beyond the lips.

Eyes
Brown, but may shade to hazel in light-coloured hounds, neither prominent nor too deep set. The expression is calm and serious and the red of the lower lid appears though not excessively.

Ears
Set on low but not excessively so and never above the line of the eye, very long, reaching at least to the end of a muzzle of correct length, narrow throughout their length and curling well inwards; very supple, fine and velvety in texture.

Mouth
The teeth level with a scissors bite, although if they meet edge-to-edge it is not a fault.

Neck
Muscular and fairly long with pronounced dewlap but not exaggerated.

Side view of head of Basset Hound

Correct

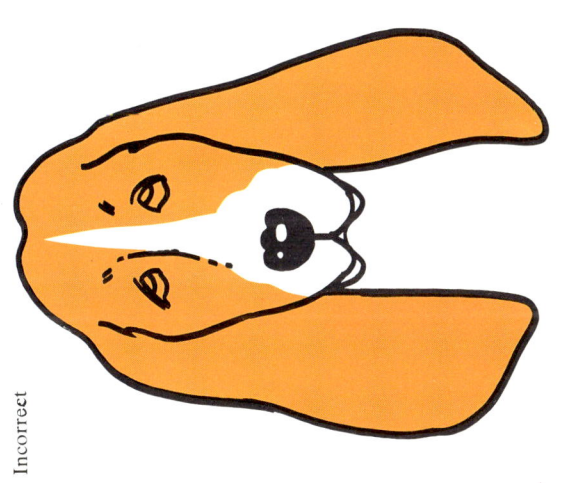

Incorrect

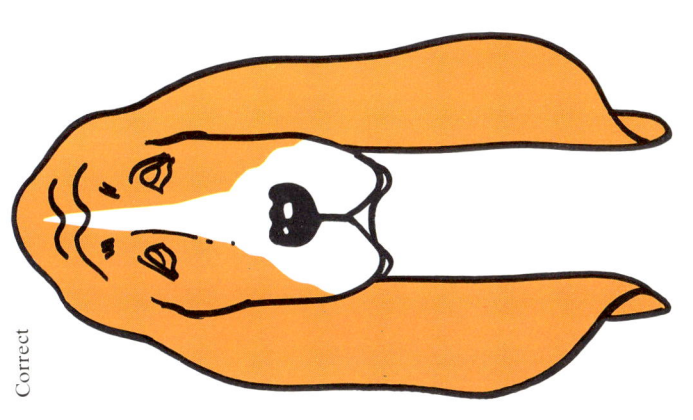

Front view of head of Basset Hound

Forequarters
Shoulder blades well laid back and shoulders not heavy. Forelegs short, powerful and with great bone, the elbows turned neither out nor in but fitting easily against the side. The knees at least slightly crooked inwards but not to so great an extent as to prevent free action or to result in legs touching each other when standing or in action. Knuckling-over is a bad fault. There may be wrinkles of skin between knee and foot.

Body
The breast bone slightly prominent but the chest not narrow or unduly deep; the ribs well-rounded and sprung and carried well back. The back rather broad, level and with withers and quarters of approximately the same height, though the loins may arch slightly. The back from withers to the inset of the quarters not unduly long.

Hindquarters
Full of muscle and standing out well, giving an almost spherical effect when viewing the hound from the rear. Stifles well bent. The hocks as low to the ground as possible and slightly bent under the hound but not turned in or out. They should be placed just under the body when standing naturally. One or two wrinkles of skin may appear between hocks and foot and at the rear of the joint a slight pouch resulting from the looseness of the skin.

Feet
Massive, well knuckled-up and padded. The forefeet may point straight ahead or be turned slightly outwards but in every case the hound must stand perfectly true, the weight being borne equally by toes with pads together so that the feet would leave the imprint of a large hound and no unpadded areas in contact with the ground.

Frontquarters of Basset Hound

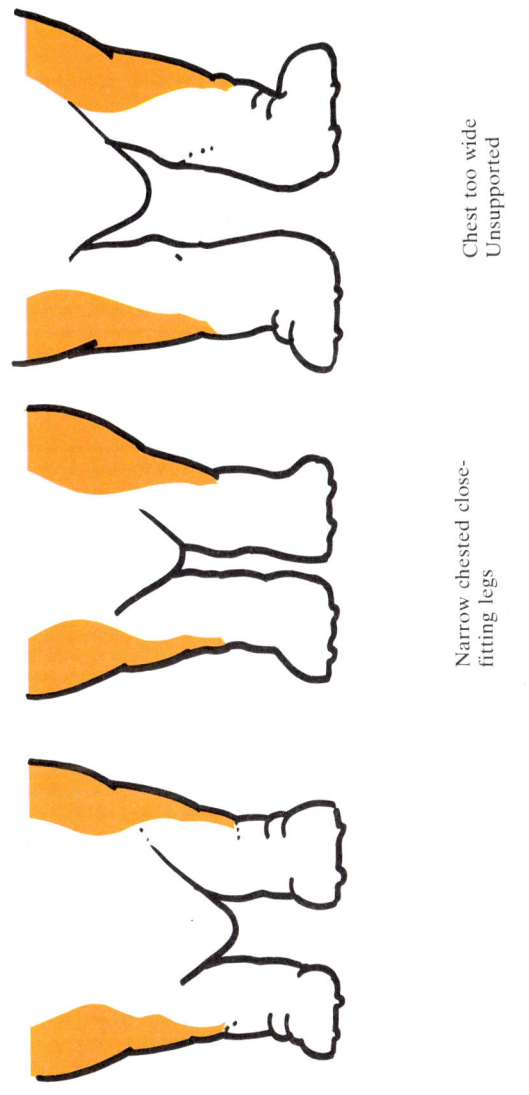

Correct

Narrow chested close-fitting legs

Incorrect

Chest too wide Unsupported

Incorrect

Tail
Well set-on, rather long, strong at the base and tapering with a moderate amount of coarse hair underneath. When the hound is moving the stern is carried well up and curves gently sabre-fashion over the back but is never curling or gay.

Coat
Smooth, short and close without being too fine.

Colour
Generally, black, white and tan or lemon and white, but any recognised hound colour is acceptable.

Height
Height 13 to 15 inches.

Faults
Any departure from the above Standard is a fault but the following should particularly be penalised:–
 (a) unsoundness of legs and feet
 (b) faulty mouth
 (c) lack of balance (i.e. undue exaggeration of any point)
 (d) lack of typical Basset appearance and expression.

(Reproduced by kind permission of the British Kennel Club)

Comments upon the Standard
The breed standard attempts to put into words the ideal attributes of the Basset but every breeder and judge's interpretation of the wording is bound to differ in detail.

In my opinion, I would put the emphasis on those sections dealing with fore and hindquarters and body at the expense of a beautiful head. I would agree with the section dealing with feet, adding that they should be surmounted by a short strong pastern and that the nails should never be allowed to grow excessively. With reference to the mouth make sure that the bite is as stated in the standard as an undershot mouth, i.e. the lower jaw protruding beyond the upper, will never right itself.

Hindquarters of Basset Hound

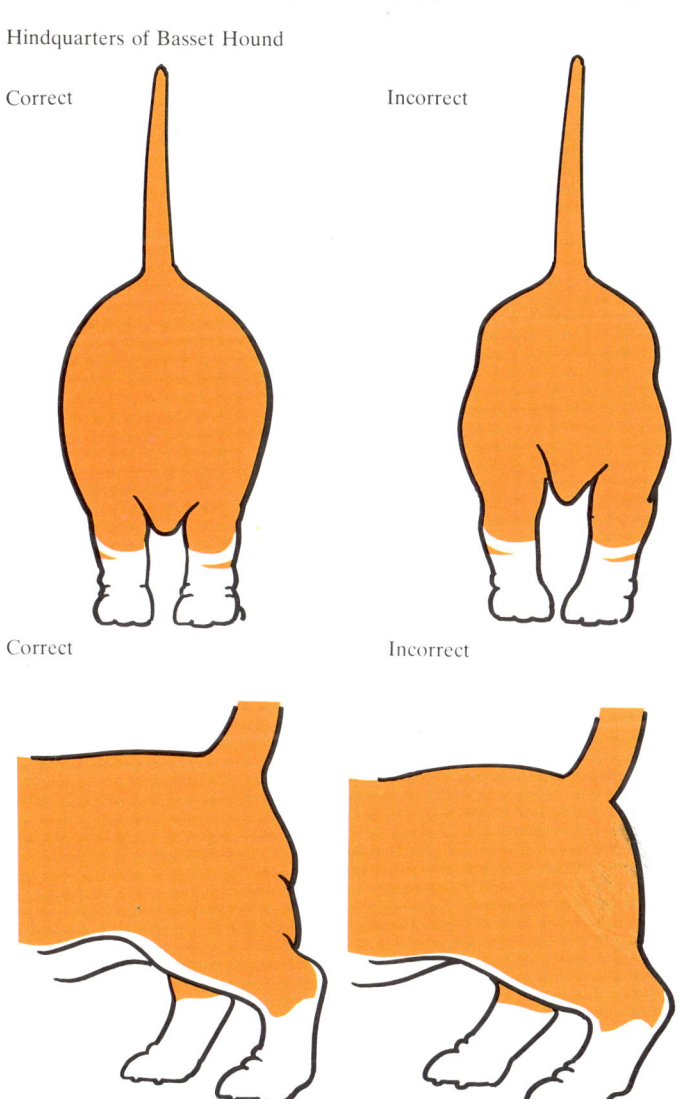

Correct Incorrect

Correct Incorrect

As the standard implies there is no completely wrong colour and both colour and markings are purely a matter of personal preference ('no good hound is the wrong colour').

Do please remember that the standard quoted above refers to a fully-matured hound and cannot possibly be applied in its entirety to an eight-week old puppy.

Meanings of some terms used in the standard

Hock – the lower part of the hind leg above the foot.

Stifle – the angle of slope of the upper thigh of the hind leg.

Occipital point – the prominent bone at the back of the skull.

Snipy – a narrowing of the foreface seen in profile towards the nose.

Flews – the loose skin hanging down over the lower jaw.

Scissors bite – the upper teeth just resting over the lower.

Dewlap – the loose skin below the jaw.

Withers and loins – the parts of the back respectively over the shoulders and hindquarters.

Stern – the tail.

Three: Choosing a Puppy

In my opinion there is only one person suited to guide a potential purchaser and that is a reputable breeder. This may involve a little travelling but it always pays off in the long run because such breeders are always willing to advise, help and pass on their accumulated knowledge regarding the rearing of the puppy of your choice.

So, first of all, if you have definitely decided that you wish to purchase a Basset puppy, either write to the Kennel Club and ask for a list of reputable breeders or contact the advertisement columns of the weekly publications *Dog World* and *Our Dogs* obtainable from newsagents. Then, make an appointment with one or a selection of breeders, go and see what they have to offer and make up your mind which type of Basset you want because every well-established breeder gradually evolves his or her own type of hound and you must choose which you prefer. If you purchase in this way, you should always be happy with your puppy and will also be able to go back to the breeder for advice and help at any time if anything should cause you concern.

Having made an appointment to visit the kennels, make sure you tell your children beforehand (as most puppies are to become family pets) that the breeder will probably ask them not to handle the puppies because, for one thing, they will not have been inoculated and you can never know whether you have been in contact with a source of infection which could be passed on via your hands. So, do respect the breeder's wishes when you are taken round the kennels. You will also be able to see the puppies' dam and very often the sire, unless an outside dog has been used. In this case the breeder will very often be able to show you a photograph of him. You can then carefully look over the puppies and probably make up your mind, bearing in mind whether you want a dog or a bitch. Many people prefer bitches – they are only a source of inconvenience twice a year and today there are numerous preparations which will help to minimize the problems. If you feel, however, that you cannot cope with a bitch at the height of her season, there should always be a good boarding kennels available in your area or probably the kennel from where you obtained your puppy would be willing to have her back during the critical period and you would then be sure that she would be in safe-keeping.

If you are early in applying to purchase a puppy from a litter, you will have a good choice, but if you should happen to be the last on the list and do not like the remaining puppy always be prepared to wait for the right one. Rushing out and buying a puppy can often be a disaster. I waited a year for my first one and it was well worth it. The breeder will show you the rest of the kennels and you will always be able to ascertain whether the dogs look fit, clean and healthy, whether their coats shine, whether the kennels are clean and you then know that you will always get a good, healthy puppy.

Personally, I never sell a puppy until it has been wormed twice, so always ask if your chosen puppy has been thoroughly wormed. All reputable breeders will give you a diet sheet to help you in rearing your puppy, because it is inadvisable to change its food at the same time as its home is changed, because environment can make a great deal of difference and the puppy will probably take a little time to adjust to new surroundings.

A healthy puppy

You may see a puppy which you like very much, but which is a little smaller than the others in the litter, but if it is lively, fit and healthy do not be put off because when a puppy settles into a new home with individual attention it very soon catches up. A good, active, sturdy little puppy is all you should ask for, but do remember that if you are buying a puppy purely for showing there is a great deal of difference between a possible show specimen and a good, strong, healthy pet. Each is good in its own way but a show specimen has extra points in its favour and this must make a difference in the price. However, many a likely champion is sitting in a back garden because its potential has not been recognised as a puppy or even has not shown its potential until it started growing out of puppyhood.

Here is a specimen diet sheet for young Bassets.

8 weeks to 6 months
Breakfast Fine puppy meal well soaked with warm milk, plus one teaspoonful of calcium phosphate powder; one of cod-liver oil.
Mid-day Raw or cooked minced meat, plus any type of vegetables (not potatoes).
Evening Same as mid-day. A little brown bread may be added.
Late evening Drink of warm milk which should be cut out at 12 weeks old. Also at 12 weeks the meat may be cut into small lumps.

6 months to 1 year
Breakfast Large-size puppy meal. Two teaspoonfuls of calcium, one of cod-liver oil.
Mid-day Cut feed out.
Evening Lumps of meat, vegetables, biscuits, etc.

1 year onwards
One meal a day – approximately 1 lb of meat, $\frac{1}{2}$ lb of biscuits.

Suitable metal feeding dishes

As the first year of a puppy's life is so important always try to give one of the meat meals as fresh meat, however cheap a cut.

IMPORTANT

Do remember that as the puppy grows, although the number of feeds is reduced, the quantities must be increased. Approximate weight of food – this is bulk weight given at each feed:
   8 weeks: 6 to 8 ozs
   12 weeks: 12 ozs
   6 months: 16 ozs
   One or two eggs may be given per week, only.
Only Regal Cream or Carnation Milk should be used – NOT COWS' MILK.

Some useful hints on rearing

DO NOT over-exercise your puppy. A romp around the garden, until he is six months, is quite sufficient. By all means lead-train him, etc. but only a little at a time in your own garden.

After the puppy has been inoculated at twelve weeks, take him out in the car with you by all means, but do not drag him around the shops nor up and down stairs. When he is fully grown, at about a year old, you may take him for as long a walk as you like.

Clean the inside of the ears once a week with round-ended tweezers and cotton wool or ear-wads. Also dry the ear if the dog has been out in the wet.

A recommended brush for grooming is a horse dandy brush.

Documents

When purchasing a puppy from a reputable breeder you should receive a copy of your puppy's pedigree (four generations) and a form enabling you officially to transfer the hound into your ownership on payment of the necessary fee to the Kennel Club. Assuming that the puppy has already been registered at the Kennel Club by the breeder, you should also be handed the registration certificate or expect to have it forwarded to you in due course if the breeder has not yet received it. Finally, you must obtain a licence once the puppy reaches the age of six months (current price $37\frac{1}{2}$p). This must be renewed annually.

Make sure also that when you take your hound out in public, there is a tag attached to his collar bearing your name and address and/or telephone number and the dog's pet name. Stray dogs brought into the Police may be put down after a week if their owners cannot be identified or contacted.

Four: Housing and Training

Before collecting your new puppy, some preparation must have been made for its reception into your home. As most puppies tend to indulge in regular chewing sessions, it is unwise to invest in an expensive dog-bed at first, unless you are sure that it is 'chew-proof'. A high-sided, stout cardboard box with one side cut down to half its own height and with a warm rug or blanket is a perfectly adequate substitute. Alternatively an enclosed, wooden puppy-box with a mesh door will ensure complete security. The main thing to ensure is that the puppy is warm and free from draughts at night. It is quite natural that a puppy newly-separated from its litter-mates will

A. A hard-wearing plastic bed

B. A canvas folding bed

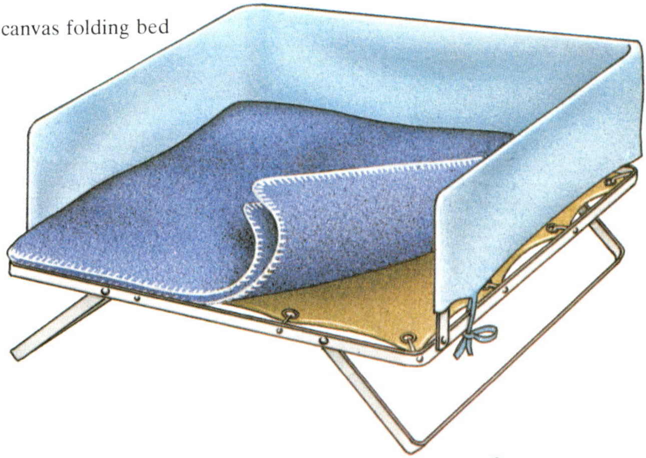

C. Home-made wooden sleeping box

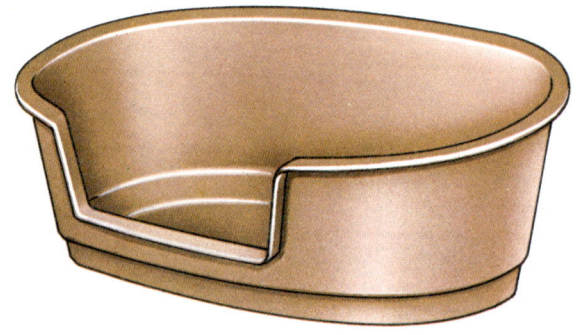

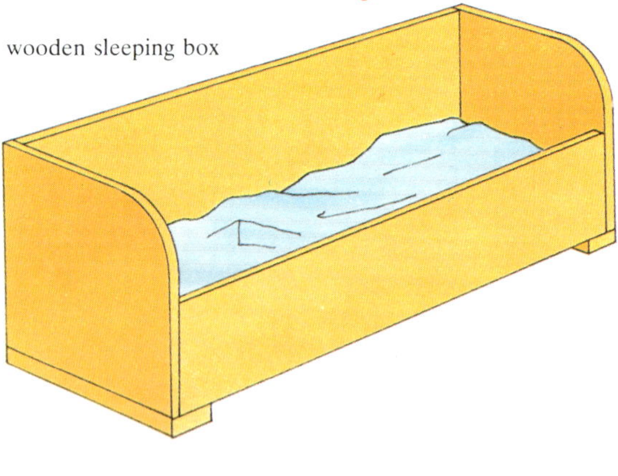

cry a little at night when first left alone, but this should not last long and should cease when it becomes accustomed to its new environment. A well-wrapped hot-water bottle, preferably a stone one, often helps to overcome the crying problem.

Training a puppy is essential from the outset and it must be taught to be obedient and clean indoors as quickly as possible as bad habits die hard. Your puppy must learn which are its own possessions – such as its bed or its toys and that it must not interfere with anything esle. A smart tap on the bottom with a rolled-up newspaper is the best means of reproof. Teaching a puppy to be clean indoors should not be difficult if tackled in the right way. Always put a puppy outside to relieve itself immediately after each feed, immediately it wakes up and, in the early stages, at hourly intervals. Always praise it when it obliges. Accidents are bound to occur, but a thick sheet of newspaper can often help indoors, particularly if it is moved nearer and nearer to the door and finally thrown outside.

A puppy showing signs of misbehaving should be placed promptly on the newspaper and again praised when it obliges.

Kennel portion of accommodation, note the air space at the eaves

In essence if you have brought up a child you are dealing with basically the same problem.

Obviously a puppy must learn the name you intend to call it by as quickly as possible and this must never be changed.

Once the puppy has got to know you, knows its name and is nearly house-trained, it is time to start lead-training. First, put on a light round collar and watch the puppy's reactions. Never leave a collar on permanently or when the puppy is on its own as accidents can quite easily happen as there are many things a collar can catch on with disastrous results. Once the puppy has become accustomed to the collar, attach a light lead. The result may well be intense resentment and a good deal of pulling and jumping about. Ignore these antics and the puppy will soon realize that they get it nowhere. Be firm, placate the puppy and try to persuade it to follow you without undue pulling. At all costs, be patient, do not lose your temper and once again, no amount of praise can be too much when the puppy does as required.

These early training sessions should be frequent rather than long and treated seriously. Preferably the same person should be in charge at all times, but with increasing success, other members of the family should be encouraged to take part.

Once basic lead-training has been successfully concluded, it is time to take your puppy out in public, but *always* on the lead and *never* before it has been fully inoculated. Obviously there will be many more distractions and interesting smells and a change to a light choke-chain collar may well be advisable as a sharp jerk on this will serve to bring the puppy to heel.

Finally, it should be possible to let your puppy off the lead when in the country or a park, but this should never be done until you are absolutely sure that it will not chase after domestic livestock or riders on horseback and that it will return to you promptly when called. A dog chasing or worrying domestic livestock can be shot and you will have no legal redress.

A. Lead and Collar

B. A slip lead

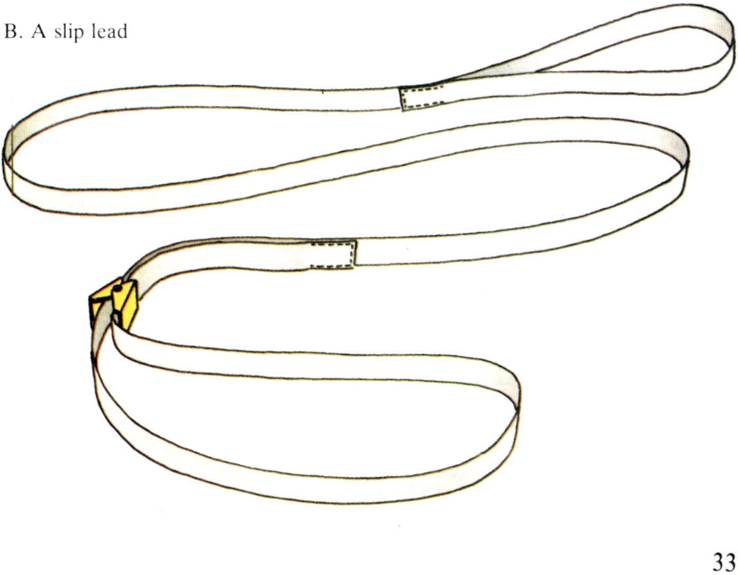

33

C. A slip lead

D. An alternative show lead

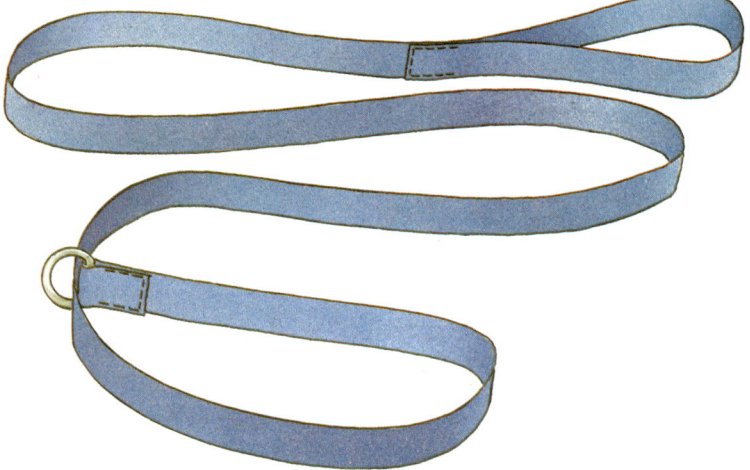

E. A check for training

Training for Show

If you are proposing to enter your puppy for shows when old enough (minimum age 6 months) further and more specialised training will be necessary before you enter the show ring (the following chapter deals with the whole question of exhibiting).

The two principal things that have to be taught in preparation for being judged at a show are:–
  (a) Submitting to being handled by the judge, and
  (b) Walking smartly to heel in a straight line and around the ring without being distracted by other dogs in the same class.

A judge will normally examine a Basset standing evenly and squarely on all four feet. Most Basset exhibitors today 'pose' or 'stack' their hounds with one hand beneath the lower jaw and the other supporting the tail at the correct angle, but there is the occasional Basset which will stand correctly on a loose lead and thus relieve the exhibitor of the necessity to get down on his or her knees, a very good thing in view of the state of the floor in many indoor rings and the physique of many exhibitors. During the judge's inspection he will always wish to examine the hound's mouth and bite and your hound must be taught not to resent this.

After examining the hound standing, the judge will normally ask for the hound to be walked either straight up and down the ring towards and away from him, or following a triangular route so that front, hind action may be assessed, and your hound must be taught to walk in the required direction without pulling, holding back or jumping about and, hopefully, 'carrying his stern gaily'.

Before taking your hound to a show make sure that his teeth, eyes and ears are clean and that nails are trimmed. Apart from grooming the coat, a Basset requires no further preparation.

In connection with all aspects of training it is well worth

attending the training classes held by most local canine societies where training at all levels is given by experienced instructors at a small charge. The dates, times and venues of such classes can be obtained from the secretary of the local society and often from your local library, recreational advice centre or local pet shops.

Five: Exhibiting

This chapter is primarily intended for the novice exhibitor having little or no knowledge of dog shows.

Often an owner of a newly-acquired Basset wonders whether it would be worth entering his hound at shows, believing that it has some show potential. Before taking the plunge, however, it would be worth asking the breeder's opinion as to whether your hound really has any prospects in the show ring as otherwise you may well spend a good deal of money without any return, financial or otherwise.

Having decided that it is really worth exhibiting, one has next to find out how, when and where to enter. Basically, there are three types of dog show. Championship Shows, where Challenge Certificates are on offer in most breeds (to achieve Champion status your hound must obtain three such Certificates under three different judges), Open and Limited Shows, the latter being restricted to members of the promoting canine society. Some shows are restricted to one or a group of breeds, while others are open to all breeds. The novice exhibitor is advised to enter first at an Open or Limited Show which will probably involve less travelling and lower entry fees.

To enter, one must obtain a Schedule listing the classes, regulations and entry fees for the show. This may be obtained from the Secretary or Show Manager of the show whose name and address will be found among the show advertisements published in *'Dog World'* and *'Our Dogs'*. On receipt of the Schedule study it carefully and decide which classes are most suited to your hound on the basis of its age and breed. Then fill in the accompanying entry form, making sure that all details are correct, referring to your registration certificate and pedigree for information regarding registered name, breeder's name, date of birth and sire and dam. Return the completed form with the correct entry fees to the show secretary in plenty of time before the closing date for entries.

Some shows are 'benched', that is provided with pens in which your hound may be secured when not required in the ring for judging. In this case you will need a benching chain to secure your hound on its bench and a rug for him to lie on while benched. At 'unbenched' shows you will have to keep your hound under control and not allow it to interfere with other exhibits.

When called by the ring steward into the judging ring, you will be told where to stand your hound and be given your ring number card or have it checked if it has already been issued. Numbers allotted to each entry will be given in the show catalogue which may be purchased at the show. This number

Basset Hound on a show bench

Basset at an unbenched show

THE SHOW RING

"Once round, please"

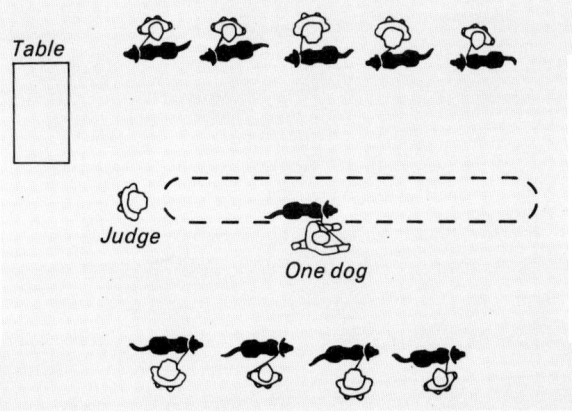

"Once up and down, please"

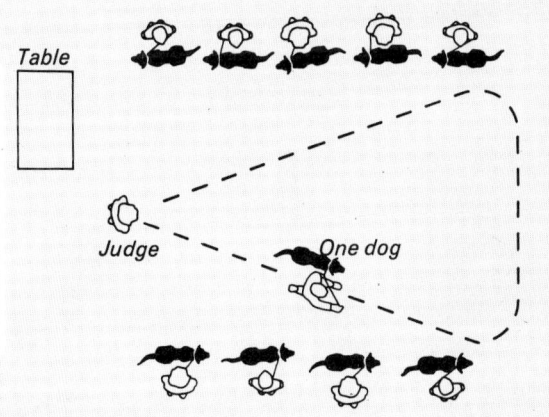

"Triangle, please"

card must be pinned to your clothing so that it is clearly visible. The judge will then examine your hound, a process which must have been prepared for prior to the show, (see under 'Training for Show',Chapter Four) and then ask you to move your hound. After all the exhibits in the ring have been examined, the winners will be called out, placed in order and awarded their prize cards. If you have entered in more than one class under the same judge, the steward will arrange those hounds already seen in order, depending on their previous awards.

What of the outcome? You may have had a marvellous day or feel that you have completely wasted your time and money. In the first case, guard against over-confidence as only in exceptional cases can you expect to always do as well. In the latter case do not be completely disheartened and give up immediately – 'another day, another judge' is a saying well worth remembering. However, if after several shows you have had no success whatever, it is best to accept the fact that your hound has not got what it takes as a show specimen while remaining a wonderful pet and companion.

Six: Your Dog's Health

Much research, time and money has gone into the protection of our pets and I always think that it is up to us to use this accumulated knowledge to the best of our advantage.

Distemper is a much-dreaded disease among dogs and it is very distressing to watch a dog suffering from it and often the after-effects are not very pleasant for the animal. Therefore, make sure that at twelve weeks of age you have your puppy fully inoculated. This also introduces him to the veterinary surgeon who will be his 'doctor' for life. At this age he may be inoculated against hardpad and distemper, or against distemper, hardpad, hepatitis and leptispirosis. These are the main ailments likely to affect a dog while young and during later life. Although years ago it was thought that one inoculation would afford protection through life, it has now been proved that it is safer to have a 'booster' inoculation every year of the same nature as the original. Without question, inoculation against distemper and hardpad at the age of twelve weeks is most important as it gives your puppy immunity against these diseases and you will be happier taking him out in public where he will come into contact with other dogs and people. At the very least, your conscience will be clear and should your dog fall ill, you have done your utmost to give him basic protection and which, in any case, is more economical these days than running up large bills from the vet due to the lack of taking elementary precautions.

During a dog's life he is sure to suffer minor cuts and abrasions, if he is very active but one does not need to call in a vet on every occasion. So always keep in your medicine chest a bottle of T.C.P. for cleansing the wound, some zinc and castor oil ointment, calamine ointment or one of the other well-known healing ointments in order that you may dress the wound yourself if it is small. If, however, it is on the large side take your dog to the vet because a large cut may require a stitch or stitches. This also applies if your dog is bitten by another. This could happen when you are walking your dog on the lead and he is set upon by another dog on the lead. Make sure you cleanse the wound thoroughly using a penicillin or other similar ointment and wash it out until you are sure that it is thoroughly clean. Finally, apply a healing ointment.

If your dog is scalded or burned it is always advisable to seek veterinary assistance, as in such cases shock is usually involved and it is very important that this should be treated professionally. In dealing immediately with the scald or burn the same measures may be adopted as with a human being, i.e. immersion in water.

Dogs often suffer from swelling of the anal glands which

can cause much discomfort and irritation around the entrance to the bowel. Such swollen glands can very easily be evacuated by your vet or if you carefully watch the procedure, you can do it yourself easily at home. Some dogs' anal glands need to be emptied two or three times a year, others perhaps only require attention once a year and some, not at all; it all depends on the make-up of the dog. The dog will give you a clue that he is suffering in this way by rubbing his bottom along the ground, continually looking round at it or even by carrying his tail down when he usually carries it up. Such signs that he is suffering in this way should not be ignored. It is also important to watch your dog's motions as any change can be an indication of a stomach upset or of something unsuitable in the diet.

It is very important to watch how your dog greets you each morning when you first meet, as he will always greet you in the same way and when he does not behave in the usual way you must look for something wrong – perhaps his eyes are a little weepy, his nose is hot or he is very lackadaisical and does not want to eat. It is a good thing in such a situation to take his temperature before getting in touch with your vet, because the first thing he will ask is what the dog's temperature is. The normal temperature for a dog is 101.6°.

It is a good idea each morning to wash out your dog's eyes with a little warm water and cotton wool. He gets 'sleep' in his eyes just as we do and he will enjoy feeling fresh again. A continual run of pus from the eye is a sign that your dog is suffering from something and this again is a case when you should take your dog to the vet who will find out what is wrong and prescribe the necessary treatment. Running eyes can also be caused by allowing your dog to hang his head out of the car window while driving which can also lead to conjunctivitis or sore eyes.

Ears should be cleaned regularly every week, or more often if unusually dirty. Some dogs do regularly get dirty ears and this is not necessarily a case of canker though often referred to as such, being usually caused by an accumulation of wax. In particular, when your dog comes in wet make sure that in addition to drying his coat you also wipe inside his ears, for stale water can cause infection.

Fits can be caused by many things but they are often associated with virus diseases or hardening of the arteries. Professional advice and treatment should always be sought straight away so that they can be kept under control.

It is always essential to keep a check on your dog's coat as fleas, lice and other parasites that live in the hair can cause skin trouble and general disability. Dusting powders will help but you can also obtain sprays or preferably bath your dog using special bathing powder prescribed by your vet.

In the summer dogs are liable to be stung by wasps or bees just as human beings are and it is essential to treat stings promptly, trying to ensure that you get the sting out. Washing soda or salt water are very useful and after the sting has been removed, treat with T.C.P. or bi-carbonate of soda. A wasp sting is often best treated with vinegar and whether stung by a wasp or a bee it is advisable to have the dog injected with anti-histamine to ensure a speedy recovery.

Eczema, which is a non-contagious disease, must be treated immediately. The dog suffers irritation and will scratch – a sore that is half the size of a fingernail at night can be as large as a 50p piece by morning! Eczema will spread very quickly and the greater degree of scratching, the greater the rate of spread. It is advisable to have this condition treated by a vet though most kennels will have their own preparations. The best way to keep a check on your dog's skin is to groom him regularly with clean brushes. Make sure you wash the brushes out thoroughly in a little disinfectant and water and rinse.

Over the years I have found that Bassets are very sensitive to draughts and this is something they cannot take. They love really cold weather and remain fit and healthy, enjoying the

Recommended Grooming Tools

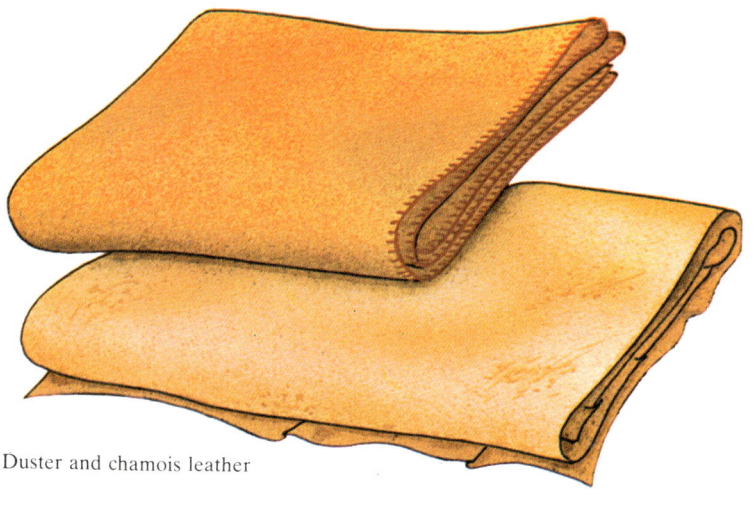

Duster and chamois leather

Dental scaler

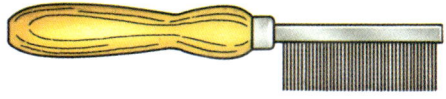

Wooden handled fine-tooth comb

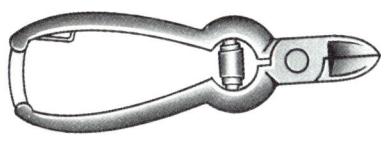

Nail clippers

Dandy brush

snow, but seem to succumb to pneumonia very easily as a result of being in draughts. Make sure, therefore, that when your dog is asleep he is not in a draught. If your dog lives outside in a kennel, it is best to have cavity walls or to have a smaller enclosed kennel inside a larger shed which will help him to generate his own heat in the smaller space.

Every spring it is advisable to give your dog a good bath in water containing a skin dressing. This will throw out all the dead hair, tone up the skin and kill any parasites remaining in the coat. Your dog should then enjoy the best of health for the rest of the year.

One good thing which your dog will enjoy is to clean his teeth once a week. A medium-hard toothbrush and a good toothpowder (I find Eucryl the best) are the best means of keeping a dog's teeth clean.

So, for your dog's care, a small cupboard or box containing a supply of cotton bandages of two different widths, a bottle of mild disinfectant, a bottle of T.C.P. or iodine, lint and cotton wool, adhesive tape, a pair of round-ended scissors, some skin ointment, canker drops, a good insecticide, packets of roundworm and tapeworm tablets for when he is older, a toothbrush and a tin of toothpowder, should be on hand.

In every case the treatment of a sick dog depends on the seriousness of the illness or injury. This determines whether you should treat him yourself or seek veterinary advice and in deciding, common-sense must always prevail.

Seven: Breeding

Before deciding to take a litter from your bitch, there are many things you must take into consideration.

Firstly, do not plan to breed a litter just because someone has told you that it does the bitch good – this is just an old wives' tale. It is a good thing only to have a litter if it is convenient to you and that the puppies will be born at the right time of the year.

As I am writing this purely for the novice, I am assuming that the reader will not know what the terms line-breeding or in-breeding mean nor about the danger of using just any dog – the latter you must certainly avoid. It is always advisable to go back to the breeder of your bitch and ask her advice. If she is a genuine and reputable breeder she will be only too pleased to help and guide you, because she will also like to see good stock to continue to be produced from her line. When I sell a bitch and the buyers go home very happy with their little girl, I always say to them that when the time comes and they are anxious to take a litter from her, to come and see me or contact me and if I have no dog that will suit their bitch, I will willingly advise them where to go because it is very important in hound breeding to breed back to the same line their bitch is bred from so that the puppies they breed will all look of the same type as one owned by them. This is the type they will wish to have as their breeding and of which they will be proud to have produced.

It is not always necessary to go to a Champion dog as this does not always mean that he will throw Champion puppies.

Basset Hound bitch and stud dog

It is much more important to use a dog that will suit your bitch. Often a dog which is very good without being a Champion will suit your bitch better and throw better puppies than one bearing a Champion title.

Now, having made the decision to breed a litter and found a dog to use which will best suit your bitch, you must then decide whether it is the right time of the year to mate your bitch. It is no use having her mated and then finding that when the puppies will be about two or three weeks old you have a holiday booked away from home, because you cannot sell puppies at two, three or even six weeks of age. They should never leave their home environment until they are at least eight weeks old and you have had time to worm them twice before they are passed on to their new owners.

The second, third or fourth season is a good time for taking puppies, that is at somewhere between eighteen months and three years of age. Do not leave it too late if you do wish to take a litter. Four years of age is almost too late and five certainly so.

Your bitch will come in season twice a year and the second or third day when she shows colour, contact the owner of the stud dog and arrange a time that is suitable both to you and to the bitch for travelling to the dog. If it is not convenient for you to travel during the week, either because your car is not available or because you cannot drive, then very often the owner of the stud dog will take your bitch in at the week-end, mate her on the right day and then you may collect her at your convenience – at least, this is what I would do.

The time for mating your bitch is usually between the tenth and the fourteenth or fifteenth day of her season; for a maiden bitch usually the twelfth or thirteenth day. Sometimes a bitch that has already had a litter is ready for mating a little earlier. There is no absolute rule regarding the correct day, it really does depend on the individual bitch when she is ovulating, but somewhere about the tenth day her season will ease up, she will be swollen and this is the time she will stand for a dog. If you press two fingers on the base of the tail and she switches her tail to the side, then she is ready for a dog and if you have booked your bitch into the stud for two or three days later, it is advisable to contact the owner of the stud dog, saying that your bitch is standing now and it will often be convenient to take her the next day. I have found through many years of experience, that there are bitches who will stand very early in their season, possibly having had the first part of the season so quickly that you have not noticed it or, on the other hand, some will stand very late, occasionally as late as the twenty-first or twenty-second day. As there is no firm rule about this, your bitch must be firmly under your eye throughout the period of her season.

At this time it is possible to administer Amplex tablets so that you do not get a following of dogs, but it is not advisable to walk your bitch out on exercise when she is in season. Lift her into the car, take her away into the country for exercise, but still do not let her off the lead, because at this critical time when she wants a dog she is likely to run off and try to find one, however obedient she normally is.

Another point I would mention here, is that some bitches do not ovulate during their season, but between seasons. Perhaps she has been off her season for three months and you will suddenly find her standing for a dog if let out loose. You could say that she was definitely not in season and I would believe you, but it can happen that a bitch mates between seasons and in due course produces a litter of puppies. This only happens in about one in a thousand cases, but you may just be the unlucky owner, although having a litter may just put the cycle right.

Once you have had your bitch mated do not think that all is over. She must still be kept under supervision for the full three weeks period and not let out loose, because having had one dog she may wish to find another. In the unfortunate event of the bitch getting out and being mismated, take her to the vet and have her injected within twenty-four hours. You should always keep a careful watch on your bitch at this time. I always keep a bitch under supervision for eight to ten days after she has finished her season and from then on, having washed her down with a mild disinfectant, all should be well.

From the time of mating onward the bitch will require careful treatment and she will need extra vitamins and such things as extra calcium, cod-liver oil or bone flour and these I advise giving as per the diet sheet for bitches in whelp below. The bitch will need these extras from the time of mating but do not increase the feed until she is five to six weeks pregnant.

I am not a great believer in a bitch being pushed and pulled about to see if she is in whelp early in her pregnancy, but a very sure sign to watch for is a change in the colour of the teats from a dead white to a glowing pink. When you see this, although there is as yet no sign of swelling, you can be sure she is in whelp and from then on take extra care that she is not bumped or knocked. Regular exercise is necessary so that the bitch goes into labour and whelps easily without having an inertia, this being usually caused through a lack of exercise.

Whelping

Whelping quarters should be as quiet as possible, warm but well ventilated and the bitch should be disturbed as little as possible. She should be introduced to the whelping quarters about ten to fourteen days before she is due to whelp. It is a good idea to feed her there from then on and leave her there for about an hour after feeding and she will soon realise that this is part of her home. The whelping bed should be a large wooden box with a rail around the inside so that she will not lie on a puppy which has crawled behind her if she lies back. The bed should be large enough for the bitch to lie out flat in both directions with a low-cut front to enable her to get in and out easily. Thick layers of newspaper should be used for bedding so that the top, soiled layers may be removed easily. She must be encouraged to move about after whelping to relieve herself as this helps the milk to flow. When the puppies are moving about straw may be used for bedding with fresh sawdust on the floor. Some form of heating must always be available to dry the puppies quickly — an overhead infrared (not white) lamp of 240w is a simple form of such heating.

A good whelping box

The normal gestation period is sixty-three days but a bitch may whelp two or three days early or two or three days late, but if she goes over the sixty-six days or becomes distressed, consult the vet immediately. A good indication that labour has commenced is a sharp fall in temperature to 99°F, shivering or scratching up her bed. You can see when the contractions start as she will strain hard and this straining becomes more frequent as the puppy comes down. During the actual whelping, the bitch should be watched carefully without being disturbed as usually she can cope with this herself, nature being what it is. However, do not let the straining go on for more than four hours without obtaining professional help. The average litter for a Basset is six to eight puppies but I have had a single puppy and I have had fifteen in a litter. There may be a long gap (between three and four hours) between the first and second puppy but with each successive puppy the time gap gets shorter and you must make sure that an afterbirth comes away after each puppy which the bitch will clear up. Even if she pants during whelping do not be tempted to give milk as this will make her sick; just see there is clean water in the corner of the kennel. Do not handle the puppies during whelping as this will worry the bitch and she will keep picking them up. She will do all the cleaning necessary. When she has finished whelping, slip her lead on and gently persuade her to come outside to relieve herself and while she is outside have the bed cleaned up and dried well before being put back with the puppies. If she appears restless after whelping and does not settle down well, have the vet check whether there is a dead puppy or afterbirth left behind and an injection will clear this up.

If the bitch does not go into labour at the appropriate time and suffers an inertia (a complete lack of labour pains) this can mean a caesarian section is required.

Only after a caesarian birth would I advise mating a bitch at two successive seasons as a mating at the season after a caesarian section usually helps to lead to a normal whelping.

Diet Sheet for In-whelp Bitches

It is important to see that right from the day of mating the

A Basset Hound bitch and her litter

bitch gets plenty of fresh meat, eggs, vegetables, calcium phosphate powder, cod-liver oil and fresh milk.

From the first week of her pregnancy the bitch should have one teaspoonful of calcium and one of cod-liver oil, on her food daily which should include at least 1 lb of meat per day. At five weeks pregnant she should be put on two meals per day. Breakfast: biscuit meal soaked in milk plus calcium and cod-liver oil. Main meal: As before (fresh meat). Three or four eggs per week may be given from the time of mating.

Feeding the bitch after whelping
She may not eat for the first twenty-four hours, so just offer her warm drinks of milk. After this she should have: Breakfast: as before. Mid-morning: warm drink of milk. Lunchtime: About 1 lb of meat, Mid-afternoon: drink of milk. Evening: Raw or cooked meat plus biscuit meal soaked in gravy. Late night: drink of milk.

Weaning puppies
Start at three weeks old; give five feeds per day. Two of 'Farex' (or similar baby food), one of milk and Ribena, one of egg and milk. Keep the mother away at first during part of the day. At five weeks old keep her away most of the day but let her sleep with them at night throughout.

7.30 am: Puppy meal with milk, calcium and cod-liver oil ($\frac{1}{2}$ tsp. of each per puppy).
11 am: drink of milk
1 pm: meat, raw green and minced carrots
3.30 pm: put mother in for fifteen minutes
6 pm: meat and vegetables
10 pm: egg and milk (one egg per three puppies)
In one feed per day add Ribena.

From six to eight weeks (increase the food per meal)
7.30 am – as before, increasing calcium to 1 tsp. and cod-liver oil to 1 tsp.
12.30 pm: meat and vegetables
5 pm: meat plus a little soaked meal
10 pm: drink of milk.

The bitch should be completely away from the puppies by six weeks old.

Puppies should be wormed at two and a half, four and a half and six and a half weeks old with Coopane Tablets as advised by Newmarket Research Hospital.

Eight: The Hunting Basset

Hunting is a sport enjoyed by people from all walks of life. At one time it was mainly country folk who hunted but nowadays towns people and city-dwellers are drawn from their concrete jungles by the sound of the horn and the cry of the hounds.

The amount of exercise taken while hunting is entirely a personal choice depending on one's health and fitness. You can follow the hounds throughout the Meet or stand on higher ground and watch from a distance with the aid of a pair of binoculars. At some Meets it is possible to follow hounds by car, catching a brief glimpse of the Pack from time to time. Whichever method is chosen there will certainly be plenty of fresh, country air to be enjoyed. During an English hunting season the followers may get cold, wet and muddy but the pleasure and excitement from a day's hunting is reward enough for the discomforts. All that is needed in the way of clothing is something warm and waterproof, together with a pair of stout comfortable shoes to cope with wet and sticky ploughed fields.

Basset hound Packs in Britain hunt the hare, an animal not to be underestimated as she is a very intelligent, agile and wily creature with a tremendous turn of speed when required. She will get up to all sorts of tricks to endeavour to throw hounds off her scent. The scent of a hare is believed to come from glands in the feet and from these glands it is deposited on the ground as she runs. It is said that the more tired a hare becomes the less scent is deposited. Scent is also affected by climatic conditions and certainly the weather is one of the factors that can determine the quality of a day's sport.

A Basset relies entirely on its keen nose to work out the line of this devious creature. The Basset is not a fast hound but has abundant stamina and perseverance to keep going at its own pace patiently seeking out the 'line' (the trail of scent) of the hare. Although the Bassets hunt as a Pack, they are independent of each other at a check (a 'check' means the hare has been up to her tricks and the scent has died). The hounds then cast back to where the scent was the strongest and slowly work out the line again. It is at this point that individual hounds come into their own and give tongue to the rest of the Pack that they have found the line. Others will check the information and then the Pack will be off on the line in full cry. A Pack of Bassets in full cry has no equal in any other Pack of hunting hounds. Their melodious voices singing out across the fields is completely exhilarating. The Basset, being low to the ground, is recognised as a low scenting animal; with this ability the Basset can provide a good day's sport even though scenting conditions may not be good. The Basset is

A model Hunting Basset

not reputed to account for a large number of hares during a season but this fact is of secondary importance to the followers, the pleasure being obtained from following the Pack and seeing them work out the line of the quarry.

A tired hare will get up to many tricks; she has been known to double back exactly on her own line for some distance and then take a gigantic leap to one side giving the hounds the impression that the line has come to a dead end. She will travel in and out of water to dilute the scent; she will go through sheep or cattle to disguise her scent; she will swim canals, dykes and small rivers. These are a few of her many tricks. Some followers consider the hunting of a tired hare to be the best part of a day's hunting as hounds are called upon to use all their abilities to work out what the wily hare has done.

Individual hounds contribute to the success of a day in the field; some are better working on roads, some do well on dry days but are not so good on wet days; some are better in a slight breeze; some work away from the main Pack (skirters) while others work closely together as a team.

There are rules to be observed when out hunting. Remember you are there by invitation of a farmer or landowner so make sure all gates are shut behind you and that no damage is done to fencing, hedges and crops. Always walk round the edge of crop fields. Do not cross the line of the hare and do not shout if you think you have seen the hunted hare; inform a member of the staff the direction in which she has gone and he can inform the Huntsman. By shouting the hounds are caused to lift their heads with the result they may lose the line at a critical point. Should you have a hound with you, keep it under control. When hunting, hounds need to concentrate and loose hounds running about can only cause them to lose the required concentration. At all times be as quiet as possible in order not to disturb hounds at their task.

Next, we come to the question – how can you introduce your hound to the joys of hunting? In England we are indeed fortunate as there is a unique Pack called The Albany Bassets which allows privately owned hounds to enter (subject to the owner being a member of the Basset Hound Club).

First of all, I will fill in some of the background to this unique Pack. About thirty years ago the Basset Hound Club was alerted to the danger of the pure Basset becoming simply a pet hound and decided to take positive steps to ensure that the hunting instinct would not be lost. A number of Club members got together (one of whom was the President, Mr Alex MacDonald) and with the help of Miss Peggy Keevil who had been hunting with the Grims Pack for some years, formed 'The Working Branch'. The aim was (and I quote) 'To foster the hunting instinct that is inherent in every Basset'. The Grims Pack was to act as a nucleus and privately owned hounds who showed promise would be encouraged to enter.

After 1969 Miss Keevil could not continue and all would have been lost had not Mr John Evans intimated that he would be prepared to kennel and keep hounds. The result of this was a newly formed 'Basset Hound Club Pack'. In 1975 they were invited to join The Master of Basset Hounds Association and one of the conditions laid down was that the Pack should change its name. As the Pack was part of the National Club it was felt the name should have some reference to Britain. After long consideration the name 'Albany' was selected this being derived from the old poetic word for Britain – 'Albion'

The Pack is under the control of the Joint Masters, a Chairman, committee and Hunt Secretary. As with other registered Packs it has registered country, in this case in West Lincolnshire where regular Meets are held. Other Meets take place in various parts of the Country through the contacts of local Club members and by invitation of local hunts, farmers and landowners.

A pack of Hunting Bassets

Should you decide you would like to join a Meet with your Basset, what should you do? First, get in touch with the Hunt Secretary who will send you a list of Meets. The usual place for meeting is the local pub in the area or from the farm over which land the Pack will be hunting. It is wise to arrive early to give you time for a chat with the Master(s) and hunt staff who will be pleased to give you any advice you need.

When you arrive at your first Meet you will see a number of members in hunt uniform. These are the hunt staff comprising the Master(s), Huntsman, whippers-in and the Field Master. Anyone who is not a member of the hunt is asked to contribute to the 'Cap'. There is a recommended 'Cap' but give what you can afford for your afternoon's sport as the money is used to help with Pack finances. Make yourself known to one of the hunt staff and let him know it is your first time out and that you are keen for your hound to enter.

You will be introduced to the Field Master who is responsible for the control of the field during the afternoon. (The followers are referred to as 'the field'). When hounds are unvanned let your hound mingle with the Pack; he may be bewildered, even a little scared at first, so stay close and encourage him. When the Pack moves off you will be asked to put your hound on a lead. From then on you will be under the control of the Field Master. Do not expect miracles at first. It may take several weeks of patience on your part before your hound has the confidence to forget you and be carried away in the thrill of the chase.

The Huntsman, by blowing different calls on the horn, can cheer hounds on or recall them with the help of his whippers-in from potential dangers (i.e. roads, railway lines, etc.) When hounds are out of sight the calls on the horn also inform the field as to what is going on and the direction in which hounds are moving. The whippers-in (more commonly referred to as 'whips') are there to assist the Huntsman, sometimes acting as forward 'look-out' to inform the Huntsman the direction in which the hare has gone. Should a whip come across a stray hound he should ensure that hound is returned to the Pack.

The Master is the person in complete charge of a Hunt. He is responsible for the breeding and management of hounds and the kennels. He is the Hunt's ambassador to local hunts, farmers and landowners. He arranges, through his secretary, the programme of Meets. It is not possible to sum up in a few words the varied duties and responsibilities of a Master. Some of these may be shared by the appointment of a Joint Master(s) and the administration side may be shared by the committee and secretary.

Although no hunting takes place during the summer months you can still help your hound to retain his instincts and get him in training for the coming Season. The Basset Hound Club has branches throughout Britain and some of these arrange walks and exercises during the summer. The exercises are intended to encourage hounds to walk together as a Pack. When hounds become used to forming a Pack, a drag may be laid. This is a trail made by a member dragging an aniseed-soaked rag or a piece of animal flesh along the ground to lay a scent. The hounds are then encouraged to follow this scent keeping to the same line as that laid. The line is over a short distance at first and lengthened as the hounds gain more experience and confidence. The walks are also valuable in helping your hound gain confidence with others. Should you live near the kennels give the Master a ring and ask for permission to take your hound along when he exercises the Pack during the summer months. Also during the closed season there is usually work to be carried out at the kennels in the way of maintenance. Volunteers for this work are always welcome. Whilst your hound may not benefit from this you will stand to gain a greater understanding of what hunting is all about.

With the Albany, if your hound shows real promise he will be awarded a 'Preliminary Hunt Certificate'. A full 'Working

Certificate' is awarded when a hound can identify and hunt a line as a member of the Pack, giving tongue only at the appropriate time. Should your hound gain a Working Certificate you will then be the proud owner of a Basset entitled to enter the Pack at any of their Meets.

Nine: The Basset Hound in America

In the United States of America the development of the breed has been similar to that in Britain, the first Bassets being officially recorded in the U.S.A. in the late nineteenth century and the first official registration being in 1885. There is, however, evidence of the breed's existence in that country in the eighteenth century, possibly introduced by the French.

In 1883 Mr George Krehl exported one of his English hounds, but interest in the breed remained generally limited until the 1920's when several wealthy Eastern gentlemen imported well-bred hounds from both England and France which provided the foundation stock for several major breeding kennels and hunting packs.

Imports from Europe declined sharply after the mid-1930's

and since then the development of the breed has very largely depended on home-bred stock and as a consequence the characteristics of the American Basset have tended to become somewhat different from those of the British hounds, making it necessary for the introduction of an official American Kennel Club breed standard appended below, which in fact, however, deviates little from the British Standard.

The chief differences noticeable in the American Basset are generally greater substance and heavier bone, slightly shorter heads with a more prominent stop and a greater depth of body.

Registrations in the U.S.A. are naturally very numerous with over 20,000 hounds being registered in 1971.

The Basset Hound Club of America was founded in 1935 and there are over twenty regional breed clubs.

In recent years some American-bred hounds have been imported into Britain and judges from both countries have officiated at Championship Shows on the other side of the Atlantic.

OFFICIAL BREED STANDARD OF THE BASSET HOUND

General Appearance

The Basset Hound possesses in marked degree those characteristics which equip it admirably to follow a trail over and through difficult terrain. It is a short-legged dog, heavier in bone, size considered, than any other breed of dog, and while its movement is deliberate, it is in no sense clumsy. In temperament it is mild, never sharp or timid. It is capable of great endurance in the field and is extreme in its devotion.

Head

The head is large and well proportioned. Its length from occiput to muzzle is greater than the width at the brow. In over-all appearance the head is of medium width. The skull is well domed, showing a pronounced occipital protuberance. A broad flat skull is a fault. The length from nose to stop is approximately the length from stop to occiput. The sides are flat and free from cheek bumps. Viewed in profile the top lines of the muzzle and skull are straight and lie in parallel planes, with a moderately defined stop. The skin over the whole of the head is loose, falling in distinct wrinkles over the brow when the head is lowered. A dry head and tight skin are faults. The muzzle is deep, heavy, and free from snipiness. The nose is darkly pigmented, preferably black, with large wide-open nostrils. A deep liver-coloured nose conforming to the colouring of the head is permissible but not desirable. The teeth are large, sound, and regular, meeting in either a scissors or an even bite. A bite either overshot or undershot is a serious fault. The lips are darkly pigmented and are pendulous, falling squarely in front and, toward the back, in loose

An American Basset Hound

hanging flews. The dewlap is very pronounced. The neck is powerful, of good length, and well arched. The eyes are soft sad, and slightly sunken, showing a prominent haw and in color are brown, dark brown preferred. A somewhat lighter-colored eye conforming to the general coloring of the dog is acceptable but not desirable. Very light or protruding eyes are faults. The ears are extremely long, low set, and when drawn forward, fold well over the end of the nose. They are velvety in texture, hanging in loose folds with the ends curling slightly inward. They are set far back on the head at the base of the skull and, in repose, appear to be set on the neck. A high set or flat ear is a serious fault.

Forequarters
The chest is deep and full with prominent sternum showing clearly in front of the legs. The shoulders and elbows are set close against the sides of the chest. The distance from the deepest point of the chest to the ground, while it must be adequate to allow free movement when working in the field, is not to be more than one-third the total height at the withers of an adult Basset. The shoulders are well laid back and powerful. Steepness in shoulder, fiddle fronts, and elbows that are out, are serious faults. The forelegs are short, powerful, heavy in bone, with wrinkled skin. Knuckling over of the front legs is a disqualification. The paw is massive, very heavy with tough heavy pads, well rounded and with both feet inclined equally a trifle outward, balancing the width of the shoulders. Feet down at the pastern are a serious fault. The toes are neither pinched together nor splayed, with the weight of the forepart of the body borne evenly on each. The dewclaws may be removed.

Body
The rib structure is long, smooth, and extends well back. The ribs are well sprung, allowing adequate room for heart and

lungs. Flatsidedness and flanged ribs are faults. The topline is straight, level, and free from any tendency to sag or roach, which are faults.

Hindquarters

The hindquarters are very full and well rounded, and are approximately equal to the shoulders in width. They must not appear slack or light in relation to the over-all depth of the body. The dog stands firmly on its hind legs showing a well-let-down stifle with no tendency toward a crouching stance. Viewed from behind, the hind legs are parallel, with hocks turning neither in nor out. Cowhocks or bowed legs are serious faults. The hind feet point straight ahead. Steep, poorly angulated hindquarters are a serious fault. The dewclaws, if any, may be removed.

(Please note: the following illustrations indicate colouring for both American and British Basset Hounds, although the shapes of the dogs are closer to those of British Breeds.)

Lemon and White Basset Hound

Tricolour Basset Hound

Black Blanket Basset Hound

Tail
The tail is not to be docked, and is set in continuation of the spine with but slight curvature, and carried gaily in hound fashion. The hair on the underside of the tail is coarse.

Size
The height should not exceed 14 inches. Height over 15 inches at the highest point of the shoulder blades is a disqualification.

Gait
The Basset Hound moves in a smooth, powerful, and effortless manner. Being a scenting dog with short legs, it holds its nose low to the ground. Its gait is absolutely true with perfect co-ordination between the front and hind legs, and it moves in a straight line with hind feet following in line with the front feet, the hocks well bent with no stiffness of action. The front legs do not paddle, weave, or overlap, and the elbows must lie close to the body. Going away, the hind legs are parallel.

Coat
The coat is hard, smooth, and short, with sufficient density to be of use in all weather. The skin is loose and elastic. A distinctly long coat is a disqualification.

Color
Any recognised hound color is acceptable and the distribution of color and markings is of no importance.

DISQUALIFICATIONS
Height of more than 15 inches at the highest point of the shoulder blades.
Knuckled over front legs.
Distinctly long coat.

(Reproduced by kind permission of the American Kennel Club)

ADDRESSES

The Kennel Club 1 Clarges Street, Picadilly, London W1Y 8AB.
The American Kennel Club 51 Madison Avenue, New York NY 10010 USA.
Dog Periodicals (Weekly)
Our Dogs, 5 Oxford Road, Station Approach, Manchester, 1.
Dog World, Clergy House, The Churchyard, Ashford, Kent.
Dog International, Eden House, 32 Well Road, Maidstone, Kent.

Breed Societies (with names and addresses of secretaries)
The Basset Hound Club
Mrs S. Hipkins, 9 Westgate Lane, Lubenham, Market Harborough, Leicestershire.

The Basset Hound Club of Northern Ireland
Mr E. Armstrong, 2 Kerrymount Avenue, Belfast BT8 4NL.

The Basset Hound Club of Scotland
Mrs B. Campbell, 'Glenview', Princes Street, Innerleighton, Peebleshire, Scotland.

The Midland Basset Hound Club
Mr F. C. Horsley, Blyth Kennels, Dexter Lane, Hurley in Atherstone, W. Midlands.

The Hadrian Basset Hound Club
Mr T. A. Sayer, 11 Salters Lane South, Houghton, Darlington, Co. Durham.

Regional Branches of the Basset Hound Club

East Anglian Branch
Mrs S. Money, 4, The Dell, Great Dunmow, Essex.

London & Home Counties Branch
Mrs H. Freeman, Tarn Hows, 13 Red Road, Boreham Wood, Herts.

Midland Branch
Mrs M. Thorley, Winney Hill Farm, Kirk Ireton, Derbyshire.

North Western Branch
Mrs N. Ledward, 10 Park Close, Whitefield, Manchester.

South Eastern Branch
Mrs H. Freeman, Fernhill Cottage, Ide Hill, Sevenoaks, Kent.

South Western Branch
Mrs R. Leaf, Peel Barton Cottage, Curry Rivel, Somerset.

Thames Estuary Branch
Mrs Betty Bicknell, Baybell Bassets, Chestnut Street, Norden, Nr. Sittingbourne, Kent.

Working Branch (The Albany Bassets)
Miss J. Blois, 26 Manchester Street, London N1.

(Intending members of regional branches must first be members of The Basset Hound Club.)

Editor's Note
The names and addresses of secretaries are those pertaining at the time of going to print.

BIBLIOGRAPHY

Appleton, D. *The Basset Hound:* Nicholson & Watson

Braun, M. *The Complete Basset Hound:* Howell Book House, N.Y.

Fitch-Dagleish, E. *The Basset Hound:* W. & G. Foyle Limited

Johnston, G. *The Basset Hound:* Popular Dogs Publishing Co.

Rowett-Johns, J. *All about the Basset Hound:* Pelham Books

Index

Page numbers in italic refer to illustrations

Albany Bassets, The 61-62, 64-65

'Basset', 8
Basset Hound Club of America, 67
Basset Hounds Club, 11, 64
'Belle', 8
breeding, 49-57
  gestation period, 54
  mating, 51-53
  suitable stud dogs, 49-51
  weaning, 57
  whelping, 53-57
  worming, 57
breed standard (Britain), 14-22
  body, 18
  coat, 20
  colour, 20,22
  ears, 15, *16, 17*
  eyes, 15
  faults, 20
  feet, 18, 20
  forequarters, 18, *20*
  general characteristics, 14
  head and skull, 14-15, *16, 17*
  height, 20
  hindquarters, 18, *21*
  mouth, 15, 21
  neck, 15, *16, 17*
  nose, 15, *16*
  tail, 20
breed standard (USA), 67-72
  body, 69-70
  coat, 72
  colour, 72
  disqualifications, 72
  forequarters, 69
  gait, 72
  general appearance, 67
  head, 67-69
  hindquarters, 70
  size, 72
  tail, 72

Canteleu, Le Comte Le Coulteaux de, 8

Champion Fredwell Varon Vandal, 11-12
Champion Rossingham Badger, 11
Clements, Mr, 9
collars, 32, *33*

dog-beds, 29, *30*

Evans, John, 62
exhibiting, 37-42
  entering, 38
  judging, 38-42, *40-41*
  types of dog show, 38

Galway, Lord, 8

health, 43-48
  anal glands, 44-45
  burns, 44
  distemper, 43
  draughts, 46-48
  ears, 28, 45-46
  eczema, 46
  eyes, 45
  fits, 46
  grooming equipment, *47*
  hardpad, 43
  hepatitis, 43
  inoculation, 43-44
  leptospirosis, 43
  parasites, 46
  stings, 46
  teeth, 48
  temperature, 45
  wounds, 44
hunting, 58-65
  joining a Meet, 63

identity tags, 28

Keevil, Miss Peggy, 12, 61, 62
kennels, *31*, 48
Krehl, George, 9, 66

Lane, Monsieur, 8
leads, *33, 34*

Masters of Basset Hounds Association, 11
Millais, Sir Everett, 9
'Model', 9

Onslow, Earl of, 8-9
origins, 7-10
  import into Britain, 8-10
  import into USA, 66-67

puppies, 23-28
  care of, 28
  diet, 25, 26
  documents, 28
  purchasing, 23, 25
  rearing, 27-28

registrations
  in Britain, 11
  in USA, 67

St. Hubert Hound, 7
Sleuth Hound, 7

Talbot, 7
training, 31-36
  classes, 35-36
  for show, 35
  house training, 31
  lead-training, 32
  uses, 10

varieties, 8, 11
  American Basset, 66-70, *68*,
  Artesian, 8
  Basset Artesian Normand, 8
  Basset Bleu de Gascoigne, 8
  Basset Fouvre de Bretagne, 8
  Basset Griffon Vendeen, 8
  English Basset, 9-10, 11
  Normand, 8